Arkansas
Facts and Symbols

by Elaine A. Kule

Consultant:
Linda R. Pine
Archives and Special Collections
University of Arkansas at Little Rock

Hilltop Books
an imprint of Capstone Press
Mankato, Minnesota

Hilltop Books are published by Capstone Press
151 Good Counsel Drive, P.O. Box 669, Mankato, Minnesota 56002
http://www.capstone-press.com

Library of Congress Cataloging-in-Publication Data
Kule, Elaine A.
   Arkansas facts and symbols/by Elaine A. Kule.
   p. cm.—(The states and their symbols)
   Includes bibliographical references (p. 23) and index.
   Summary: Presents information about the state of Arkansas, its nickname, motto,
and emblems.
   ISBN 0-7368-0634-2
   1. Emblems, State—Arkansas—Juvenile literature. [1. Emblems, State—Arkansas.
2. Arkansas.] I. Title. II. Series.
CR203.A84 K85 2001
976.7—dc21   00-021413

Editorial Credits
Erika Mikkelson, editor; Linda Clavel, production designer and illustrator;
   Heidi Schoof and Kimberly Danger, photo researchers

Photo Credits
Arkansas Department of Parks and Tourism, 10
Bruce D. Flaig, 20
KAC Productions/Bill Draker, 12
Karlene V. Schwartz, 14
Kent and Donna Dannen, 22 (top)
One Mile Up, Inc., 8, 10 (inset)
Robert McCaw, 18
Root Resources/Garry D. McMichael, 22 (middle)
Unicorn Stock Photos/Tom Edwards, 16
Visuals Unlimited/Barbara Gerlach, cover; Henry W. Robison, 6; Mark E. Gibson, 22 (bottom)

1 2 3 4 5 6 06 05 04 03 02 01

Table of Contents

Capital: The capital of Arkansas is Little Rock.

Largest City: The largest city in Arkansas is Little Rock. More than 175,750 people live there.

Size: Arkansas covers 53,183 square miles (137,744 square kilometers). It is the 27th largest state.

Location: Arkansas is in the south central United States.

Population: The population of Arkansas is 2,551,373 (U.S. Census Bureau, 1999 estimate).

Statehood: On June 15, 1836, Arkansas became the 25th state to join the United States.

Natural Resources: Petroleum, natural gas, and the chemical bromine are important natural resources in Arkansas.

Manufactured Goods: Workers make color TVs, plastic products, and furniture in Arkansas.

Crops: Farmers in Arkansas grow rice, soybeans, and cotton. They also raise cattle and chickens.

State Name and Nickname

French explorers arrived in the area that is now Arkansas in 1673. They asked Algonquin-speaking Native Americans to guide them. The Algonquins called the nearby Quapaw Indians "Arkansea," which means "people of the south wind." The French used the name Arkansea for the Quapaw and the region.

People spelled and pronounced the name Arkansas many ways. Arkansas was the spelling when it became a state in 1836. In 1881, officials decided the state's name should be pronounced AR-kan-saw.

From 1953 to 1995, Arkansas's official nickname was "Land of Opportunity." Officials gave the state this nickname because they hoped it would bring industries to Arkansas. In 1995, the legislature changed the official nickname to "The Natural State." Arkansas is known for its beautiful lakes, mountains, and wildlife.

Tumbling Falls waterfall is in the Ozark Mountains. The Ozark Mountains are in northern Arkansas.

State Seal and Motto

State officials adopted the state seal in 1864. The seal represents Arkansas's government. It also makes state government papers official.

An eagle is in the center of the seal. An angel stands to the left of the eagle. The word mercy is written across her dress. The word justice appears on a sword to the right of the eagle. These symbols remind the government to be kind and fair to its citizens.

The eagle has a shield on its chest. Pictures of a steamboat, a plow, a beehive, and wheat appear on the shield. These symbols show how the people of Arkansas earn money.

The Goddess of Liberty stands above the eagle. A ring of stars surrounds her. She holds a pole in one hand. A wreath of victory is in the other. The goddess represents freedom.

A ribbon with the words "Regnat Populus" is in the eagle's beak. State officials adopted this state motto in 1907. These Latin words mean "The People Rule."

Arkansas officials added the state's motto to the seal in 1907.

State Capitol and Flag

Little Rock is the capital of Arkansas. Arkansas's capitol building is in Little Rock. Government officials meet there to make the state's laws.

Workers began building the capitol in July 1899. They built the capitol with limestone and marble. Workers finished the building in 1915.

The state's flag flies above the capitol. Arkansas officials adopted the flag in 1913. The flag is red, white, and blue. The white diamond on the flag shows that Arkansas is the only diamond-producing state. The 25 stars show that Arkansas was the 25th state to join the United States.

Three blue stars below the state name represent the three nations that ruled Arkansas. France made the first permanent settlement in 1686. Spain occupied the land in 1800. In 1803, the United States bought the area from France in the Louisiana Purchase. Officials added a fourth star to the flag above the state name in 1923.

The limestone used to build Arkansas's capitol building came from northern Arkansas.

State Bird

Arkansas's state legislature adopted the mockingbird as the state bird in 1929. Arkansas's State Federation of Women Club suggested the mockingbird.

Mockingbirds are songbirds. They change the tune of their song often. Mockingbirds also can copy, or mock, the sounds of other birds and noises they hear.

More than 30 kinds of mockingbirds live throughout the United States and in parts of Canada. The most common type is the northern mockingbird. It has a white breast and a gray coat. The bird's wings and tail are dark gray with white markings.

Mockingbirds build their nests in bushes and low trees. They lay four to six eggs in the spring. The eggs usually are blue to green-blue with spots.

Mockingbirds help farmers by eating insects and weed seeds. But mockingbirds sometimes eat fruit and destroy fruit crops.

Some mockingbirds can imitate sirens, barking dogs, and pianos.

State Tree

The Arkansas legislature voted to adopt the pine as the state tree in 1939. The pine grows in many areas of Arkansas.

Pine trees are evergreens. Evergreens stay green all year. Green, pointed leaves called needles grow on pine trees. Cones grow on the tree. The cones are 4 to 8 inches (10 to 20 centimeters) long. Some pine trees grow to be 100 feet (30 meters) tall. The pine tree has a long, straight trunk.

Two groups of pine trees grow in the United States and Canada. One type is soft pine. Soft pines have soft wood. Pitch, or hard, pines have hard wood. Several species of pine trees are in each group.

The most common pine tree found in Arkansas is the loblolly. It has long, sharp needles and large cones. Loblollies grow in Arkansas's Ouachita (WOSH-i-taw) National Forest and the Ozark-St. Francis National Forest.

The bark on a loblolly pine is dark brown.

State Flower

The apple blossom became Arkansas's state flower in 1901. Women's clubs in Arkansas held a contest to choose the state flower.

Apple blossoms have pink and white petals. The blossoms appear on apple trees in spring and soon fall off. Apples grow on the trees after the blossoms fall off.

Arkansas once was the nation's leading apple producing state. Orchards grew mostly in northwestern Arkansas. In the late 1800s, Arkansas's apples often won prizes at fairs.

In the early 1900s, diseases killed many of the apple trees in Arkansas. At that time, other states began to grow apples. The state of Washington now produces the most apples. But some Arkansas farmers still plant apple orchards. Every year, the people of Lincoln, Arkansas, hold the Arkansas Apple Festival.

Apple blossoms have pink or white petals. Apples grow on the trees after the blossoms fall off.

State Mammal

Arkansas's legislature named the white-tailed deer the state mammal in 1993. The white-tailed deer lives in many areas of Arkansas.

The white-tailed deer looks much like other deer. The deer has thin legs and black hooves. Its eyes are large and brown. The deer has smooth, shiny fur. Its fur is red-brown in summer. In winter, the deer's fur is blue-gray.

The white-tailed deer's tail is white and fluffy. The deer raises its tail when it is afraid.

White-tailed deer spend much of their time looking for food. They eat the buds and twigs of trees and bushes.

The white-tailed deer was important to the early Arkansas settlers. The settlers hunted the deer for food and made clothing from deer hides.

Male deer have antlers. Every year, the male white-tailed deer sheds its antlers and grows new ones.

More State Symbols

State American Folk Dance: Officials adopted the square dance as the state American folk dance in 1991. Square dances contain many steps. A square dance caller usually calls out the steps during the dance.

State Beverage: Government officials chose milk as the state beverage in 1985. Dairy farming is an important part of Arkansas's agriculture.

State Insect: In 1973, officials chose the honeybee as the state insect. Beekeepers gather and sell the honey made by the bees. A beehive is one of the symbols on Arkansas's state seal.

State Gem: The diamond became the state gem in 1967. Arkansas is the only diamond-producing state in the United States. The Crater of Diamonds is a state park in Murfreesboro, Arkansas. Visitors have found more than 70,000 diamonds there.

Honeybees make honey by sucking nectar from flowers.

Blanchard Springs Caverns

Blanchard Springs Caverns are located in Arkansas's Ozark National Forest. The caverns were discovered in 1963. Visitors take guided tours of the caverns. Visitors also hike along trails and swim in the natural pool.

Crater of Diamonds State Park

Crater of Diamonds State Park is in Murfreesboro. Visitors dig for diamonds and other gems on the 36-acre (15-hectare) field. They may keep the diamonds or gems they find. People also hike on trails and camp in the park.

Ozark Folk Center

The Ozark Folk Center is in Mountain View. The center shows the mountain culture of Arkansas's early pioneers. Visitors take workshops to learn about pottery, candlemaking, and weaving. Each evening, musicians perform concerts featuring Ozark folk music.

Words to Know

agriculture (AG-ruh-kul-chur)—producing crops, raising livestock, and other farming activities

cavern (KA-vurn)—a deep hollow place underground

crop (KROP)—grain, fruit, or vegetables grown on the land

legislature (LEJ-iss-lay-chur)—the part of the government that makes laws

liberty (LIB-ur-tee)—freedom

marble (MAR-bul)—hard stone used for making buildings

natural gas (NACH-ur-uhl GAS)—a gas found beneath the earth's surface; it is used for heating and cooling.

petroleum (puh-TROH-lee-uhm)—a thick, oily liquid found below the earth's surface; petroleum is made into gasoline.

species (SPEE-sheez)—a group of plants or animals that share common characteristics

Read More

Altman, Linda. *Arkansas.* Celebrate the States. New York: Benchmark Books, 2000.

Kummer, Patricia K. *Arkansas.* One Nation. Mankato, Minn.: Capstone Books, 1999.

Welsbacher, Anne. *Arkansas.* The United States. Minneapolis: Abdo & Daughters, 1998.

Useful Addresses

Arkansas Department of Parks and Tourism
One Capitol Mall
Little Rock, AR 72201

Arkansas State Capitol Building
Little Rock, AR 72201

Internet Sites

Arkansas Home Page
http://www.state.ar.us
Arkansas Parks and Tourism
http://www.arkansaskids.com
Arkansas State Symbols
http://www.50states.com/arkansas.htm

Index

Made in the USA
Las Vegas, NV
17 December 2020

Another way to keep the practice fun and fresh, after you've read this book over and over with your little ones, is to have them tell you the story back, using the pictures to guide them.

Want a fun way to practice these tongue movements? Songs like "Baby Shark", "The Itsy Bitsy Spider", and "Twinkle, Twinkle Little Star" have a lot of the T/D/N sounds in them. Another movement that can help get their tongue tips moving better is having them practice scraping their tongue along the roof of the mouth (I tell them to pretend they have peanut butter stuck there and have to scoop it off with their tongue).

If your child has trouble getting the tip of their tongue up to the roof of their mouth, they may have ankyloglossia (tongue-tie) where the web of tissue under the tongue is thicker or shorter than usual. This can be diagnosed by a physician or a dentist.

These books are not intended to be a substitute for skilled speech therapy treatment. They are meant to be a supplemental addition to practice at home, and a way for families to work together on early sound production activities. If you are concerned about your child's speech, please ask your school system and your pediatrician for a speech therapy evaluation.

Don't forget to stop by our website for free songs and crafts to pair with our P.A.C.B. Speech book series.

FOR MORE INFORMATION ON SPEECH SOUND DEVELOPMENT AND HOW READING IMPACTS SPEECH DEVELOPMENT, VISIT: HTTPS://WWW.PACBSPEECH.ORG/HOME CHECK US OUT ON INSTAGRAM! @P.A.C.B.SPEECH

Helpful Tips for Parents:

One of the best parts of T, D, and N is how visible they are as we say them. As long as we exaggerate the movement, kids can see what our mouth is doing to create them. A great way to help your child learn these sounds is to pause and ask them to watch you say it. I like to say, "Watch how I say it," and tap the center of my upper lip to get their attention on my mouth before I say the word. For T, D, and N, I start by tapping the same spot at the center of my upper lip just as my tongue tip goes up for the sound.

I only have them practice the sound in isolation (not in the word) on one page in this book (Ta, Ta, Ta), because we don't want the pre-word sound practice to become a habit.

Did you know that vision and hearing problems greatly impact speech learning? If your child is struggling to produce sounds, reduced vision or multiple ear infections may be a factor. This is something to bring up to your pediatrician.

For younger children and children with delayed speech sound production, practicing their speech can be very frustrating. Even when they don't get a sound right, positively praising their efforts can make them feel good about it. "I like how hard you're working" or "you're getting very close, great job" are good ways to praise their efforts, even when they don't hit the target sound perfectly.

This book offers over 200 chances to practice sounds made by the tips of the tongue (called alveolar sounds), making it great for speech sound development and practice at home.

About the Author: Cass Kim

Cass Kim is an established young adult author. She is best known for creating the "Autumn Nights" Charity Anthology Series, as well as the "Wilders" Young Adult trilogy. In addition to her work as an author, Cass is a practicing Speech-Language Pathologist with a decade of experience. She holds her Certificate of Clinical Competency from the American-Speech and Hearing Association, as well as a master's degree from Central Michigan University.

About the Illustrator: Kawena VK

Kawena VK grew up in Hawaii with a great fascination for art and nature. She learned through a traditional atelier at the Windward Community College where she was inspired, by her college instructor, to pursue art. She later received her Bachelor of Arts from the University of Hawaii. With her family and friends, Kawena has found a deep sense of happiness through her love for drawing and painting.